The Life Of a WANNABE A MOGUL

MENTAL DiSARRAY

A Book Written By Bella Thorne

RARE BIRD
Los Angeles, Calif.

THIS IS A GENUINE RARE BIRD BOOK

Rare Bird Books
453 South Spring Street, Suite 302
Los Angeles, CA 90013
rarebirdbooks.com

Artwork by Mod Sun and Dani Thorne
Back Cover Artwork by Žaneta Bad'urová

FIRST PAPERBACK EDITION

For more information, address:
Rare Bird Books Subsidiary Rights Department
453 South Spring Street, Suite 302
Los Angeles, CA 90013

Printed in the United States

10 9 8 7 6 5 4 3 2 1

Publisher's Cataloging-in-Publication Data
Names: Thorne, Bella, 1997–, author.
Title: The Life of a Wannabe Mogul: Mental Disarray /
A Book Written by Bella Thorne.
Description: First Paperback Edition | New York, NY; Los Angeles, CA:
Rare Bird Books, 2021.
Identifiers: ISBN 9781644281185
Subjects: LCSH Thorne, Bella, 1997–. | American Poetry. |
BISAC POETRY / American / General
Classification: LCC PZ7.T3923 L54 2019 | DDC 811.6—dc23

I dedicate this book to none other than My. Muthafukken. Self.
& all the lovely lost souls out there.

INTRO

so i wrote two books that i was making
into one. guess what i did??

i left them on a fucking delta plane.
round
so i was on my last notes on the book

keep in mind its all HAND WRITTEN
who even hand writes shit anymore?

this girl (thumbs up
emoji)

i looooovve me some old fashioned pen and paper
god it feels weird saying that. i wonder
if our parents , that generation right before
us , ever thought pen and paper in this day
in
age would be referanced as old fashioned
anywhoo enough—wh— with the story telling stalli

long story shorts—
since i left the whole 2 books on the plane
i wrote a whole new one for you
thats vastly different than the other two.
i wonder if someone will ever read those
books or if the y are lost in the abyiss

never to be appreciated.

when life gives you lemons
you throw rocks at youself.
because
FUCCCKKK MEEEE why didnt i photocopy
it like mod said. GD. i guess ill have to

take that whole

" life happens as its meant to be "

thing to the grave.

welcome to mental dissaray vol. 1

inside

the mind of a wanna be mogul

THE LIFE OF A WANNA BE MOGUL

wait scratch that part out

did you scratch it?

THE LIFE OF A ~~WANNA BE~~ MOGUL

. . . .

yeah imma make that shit

happen

2/2

im not fixing my imperfections

for your idea of perfect.

so if you dont like how i do

things, or how i say things

or how i spell things.

you can kindly fuck off

sersiouly,
drop this book in the trash &

never talk about it again.

because i am not worth your idea of

perfection i never will be

i am not worth your idea of a perfect

time and neither is this book.

bye now.

ps. i only use punctuation for feeling

purposes..

identity

handwriting is a form of your true identity.

nothing hiding, no masks up.

finally just a bit-a- a peice of your true being.

handwriting can tell youso much about a person

where they might be from, what shoes they might like,

how they might prefer their room, what the inside

of thier brains might feel like..

maybe thats why i lost the first books.. because they
were hand written ... maybe im not supposed to reveal
my true identity yet...

i also think thats wha-- why autographs are such a good momento
like just a written name is nothing really..but something that was tou hed
that was sat over and tought about thats an auto graph.. thats hand writing

thats just a bit of their true idenity.
my hand writing tells a good amount of my true me.

its quite messy and scratchy, with a flare of sweet all natural sugar
almost like a childs writing ... but well.. a really messy child.
my mom used to call it doctors writings.. huh..
you can tell through my handwriting just how scattered my brains are
scar
scattered like noodles in spagetti.
where as my sisters handwriting is beautiful and neat, almost girly
you can very much tell how organized of a person she is.

it would be eaiser to explain if i just showed you our rooms..

So what does your hand
writing tell you???

some may call it ~~add~~=

ADD
i call it the signs of a
creative mind.

i just want to make you happy

so i forget to make myself happy.

how could

you not tell
me that you

told her?

given our whole

life & now its

all over.

throwing our chanes

chan ces away. like
grains to the sand
i thought time would wash us
away but instead shes

spalttered us like rocks over
looking the bay.

the
ashes that
lie ar ound
bathe broken ba
bay are the

peices th-
left for us to
pick up this may
screates and
lies are the

childs cries...

the most fucked

up
part is
every th time
i think of you
i fart.
had to get ty

that cheeky
line in beca
i figured this
dark shit was

no longe-
charming
you see

why ar
u st

ne ct of

the act of knowledge

th e act of knowledge

knowledge can be described in many ways.
    i guess the question is in which form of knowledge
    is your cream of the creme
which form of knowledge suits you best??

    ill start with my form of knowledge ,

        my form of knowledge is being taught,

            knowing the difference between right and wrong,
                up and down, and if the world is
                    ound or flat.

    thats my perfect idea of knowledge but yet

        thats not acctually my form of knowledge

        the knowledge that i know to be my trust====
                                   truth
is when the trees shake i wonder if they are
        crying for a better world around them,

        the knowledge if i say one more thing and
        push this edge , the walls might shatter

        the knowledge of knowing that ill never have the
        knowledge of truly understanding the ground
        beneath us and how it came about.

the knowledge of knowing the stupidity one might spend their whole
    life waisting the true moments they live in, just to have the
    fleeting knowledge that no one, no being can state

            for a true fact.

yum

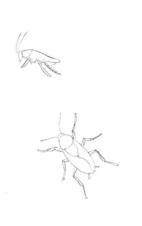

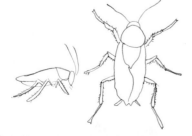

the insects are here
    fear the near the end is here.

```
                love love* love love love
            love love love lo elove love love love
             love he*elove
                   love   love hate hate you fucking bastard
                 love lov    hate
              love
                    love love
            love*ove    hat*ate love love love love
                            love love hate
                 hate
      love love        you stupid fucking bitch love
  hate hate love love love*ate hate hate hate       hate hate love
        love      hate
             love love   the power of being love
      love          stupid fuking ucuntcuntcuntcuntcuntcuntcuntcuntcunt

                   love love love i love you love love
         love my heart is black
              hate     hate          love love love
 love          hate       hate   love
     love         hate    hate   love   you love the wrong way darling...
         love love      love hate
     have       hate   love
         love hate    love     she raised me with this love
                love   hate all          love
           hate you liar     the     same        i love you
                         liar      love
         love      love          liar liar
                                        my truth
```

sours and blues
charcoal dark as night
peak around the corners
one wrong step and he will

bite.

move far from the ledge.
or you might fall with a fright.
dream of whats left and tonight
will be the night.

now close your eyes.

did you
see him?

selfish

im selfish, i can be selfish

at least i can admit it.
what
what makes a person selfish
in your eyes? is it simply
not doing things

for others when you know it can help

them? is it the way that guy wears
tie or the way that girl does her hair?
is it not putting yourself in an
uncomfortable situation to help others?

OOOOOORRRRR.....RRRRRRR.RRRRRRR RRRRRR

is it just not giving one fuck

about anyone or anything but yourself???
mmmmmmmm im guessing you think its all 3 of those thi
so whatever you can call me selfish , im accepting

im a selfish person. i was molested my whole young

life, and when i talk to other victims that havebeen

sexualy abused, they all say different things. no story is ever

the same but theres usually similaritys, they all hate, despise

their aattackers but me? no i dont hate him. does that make me

disgusting? does it make me a terrible person , knowing hes out there

maybe doing it to someone else and im not stopping him. im not saving her

you wonder why im not. my ex, he was the first person i really fully told

he kinda emotionally beat it out of me, and his response? furous, i was so shocked becau

" we need to throw him in pirson." i was so shocked. i was so shocked because

he hated him. hearing one story and he htd him with every feeling in his

body. one story. so why didnt i why dont i wanna get him into trouble

why dont i want him to pay for all the pain hes caused.

he didnt have to deal with the countless times he molested me,
he didnt deal with the countless times i felt ashamed or disgusting,
and he already hated him. so why?

i think stock home syndrome is why. putting trust or love into your
captour because its the only way you can deal with the situation in front

of you. the only way i could deal with it i guess, is by loving it
loving this cruel nature of his. hating what he was doing to be
but trying to conviced- myself that i loved it,

because i was letting it happen to me. i wasnt kicking his teeth in
i was just simply letting it..... happen to me. so how can i sit here
and write thisand do nothing about it.
                    because
                          i
                            am
                              selfish

i dont want to sit down with the cops and cconvice them i was raped many times
why should i have to convice someone i was taken advantage of?
why is our legal system so fucked up they make their victims feel like villains
they sit there smug and try and convice you , YOU were askin g for it.
im sorry no. i was not sixxx years of age asking for this cruelity.
no girl was drunk at a party asking to be raped, defiled.

i dont care if you didnt SCREAM no. that doesnt mean you werent raped.
that doesnt mean thats- whats happened to you is nothing.

guess it just means what happened to you, they dont understand it.
ostliekly because they havent exs experienced it.

i just dont wanna hope anymore hope-ee--- people will do the right thing because
havent im taking that blame. im not hiding im no coward. but yet i am.

because im lucky enough to be in a country where i have the right to speak my
mind. when i first started writing this peice i thought yes im definitely
selfish, but im not im just lost , and i need to give myself the chance not
                    to be selfish

              wish me luck.

2/2

hen right is wrong
    and they sky was born black
        runaway because the gold monster will chase you far away
            back to the great golden sack
                then you will wake up bright and new
                    given a new chance to get the day back
                        but fear the near
                            because the golden monster will be back.

what happened to your face?
    i tried to cut my own eye open with
a box cutter.
    whats it look like ?
    a cat scratched me.

accepting acceptance

what the fuck is wrong with me?

why do i always need validation from everyone around girls
    people, people i dont even know! !! shit fucking animals

      i need god damn validtion from a fucking ccricket crossing
    the road. but mostly the vaildtion that feels the most grody is
    the one i need from men....

be alone! be single! love yourself! make yourself happy!

but all those things sound really fucking scary to me.

i just need him to tell me its ok, i need him to be there for me,

when the waters are rough. i want him to love me to look me in the eyes

    and say "your e- accepted. i accept you bella"

          why?? because i cant accept myself.

    for some reason in my head im just not fucking good enough.

not good enough for him or them or anyone for that matter.

ans since i cant have him i just look for the next him or the next her
why cant i just look for the next me. find me and accept me.
    was it beacuse i was molested my whole life?

    exposed to sex at such a young age that feels the most natural to

offer the world? or is it because i was raised to think i wasnt good

enough? god im sure a really good therapist would have a great answer
for me but all i have is this paper and this type writer.

so i guess i think im just not good enough, not good enough for him or her

none of this matters , what happeneed to me. what matters
    is whats happening to me right Now, i cant blame my childhood
        in fact i cant oblame anyone for any thing .

            all i can do is blame me.

i blame X me for not loving myself,
i blame me for thinking im not attactive,

    i blame me for putting this on everyone around me.

1/2

expecting people to love me enough
for
me to love myself. thinking if someone loves me
enough i wont forget to love myself.

but at the end of the day that will never happen

because the only way to get to your end goal

is to work through it.

not above or around, or try to find a cheat code to level
up so you dont hurt as bad. you have to hurt in this world

hurting loving, and accepting . thats what our

emotional world lays on.

theres a lot of one of these going around right now.

can y ou guess what it is? ——————— ur answer here

hurting. right now theres a lot of hurting.

and right now im only hurting myself.

by not loving me and accepting me, usally these free handed writing

bits they have an end, a conclusion.

but this one doesnt have an end . im still ifiguring this one out,

as always. so is that ok? is it ok to know what your end goal is
but absolutely no idea how to achieve it..??

probably not, but i can only start by

accepting it.

tana tana tana

YOU BEAUTIFUL BABY

WHEN WILL YOU EVER LEARN

YOU GIVE THE WORLD ENOUGH

JUST FROM LIVING HERE.

YOU TASTEFUL LADY

WHEN WILL YOU EVER LEARN

YOUR MIND IS ENOUGH
BUT YOUR BIG BEHIND STOPS TRAFFIC
MY DEAR.
CRAZY BABY WILL YOU STAY WITH ME MAYBE?

is of no knowledge to your 2 eyeys
is ia
somehow whats seemingly
right in front of us
but is exploitative & showered in gold
in ur 3rd

aCokecian cokecain

whyy dont they put cokecain in coke anymore
man that was fun.

—general consumption in America, 1904

i i cant wait to have kids   kdskidskids   /18

               iln   g kids ids ids
i ha c at i   o have kids

    i ha h   hjjjj

    i cant wait to h ve kids

        i ha hearing t hat phrase
              " he thought having kids would make her happy"
              "some relatively new to love douche b g ays"
        i cant im gine a life i my mid 0s w out kid on my arm
        i hon stly gnun ley beli ve havin kids   W ULD fix ll my problems..
       b cause the only problem t at needs fixin is my sadness.
       but if i n d no her individu l th t shares this l ve with me just then...
       just th n MAYBE i could be happy. finally i would have something 2 care
       about t

       about fully inste d of   letting the sel-fish ways of society that we are
       t-ug t
       promin ntly con ide   ith y f elin s..
       i just k ep th king...
just k s working o hard 2 m ke sure
       i can re th m h t vever hey need bocome hoever they re..
       i f el th t th n th ir happiness lmus   b come your h ppiness..
nd i not dipshit i know or at leastb i assume ha   kids isnt all
rainbo s and pi k ummie bears ss   hetimee but it se m as if no hing
       that wo ld ever o wron   ould make me regret having hese w ond rful
              bunn s of joy.
       i just cant see that happening.
       o   xo   i j st wont let that happen
     OR CRATBEE
OR AYBE I REFUSE   t o share any ounce of regret that would lay around
my
finding its path 2 resent ment in my heart.
       bec use an ounc of re -t -- regret towards the only thing you
       e er did right in your life.. .ell maybe that

                    could destroy a person
                        nside out .

i see theres nothing we can do

i wish my heart had a place that

lies especially for you

but i dont thats not true ,

down in the gutter well
take another 2
i see the ending road but im not sure
t heres a shadow
for me
and you.

so ill say goodbye theres no reason to try

when your already blue oo

but i dont mind ill love the color
blue because thats the color of
you.

down in the gutter spit out another
one last chance lets die together

and love forever

in beded in each other

depresi n depres ion
depression depression
depression depression depression

the feeling of being numb to existene.

some one could hold you as tight as they can
and somehow youll still feeling that chilling
that chilling breeze running up your naked
back.

holding you so tight till theres no one
breath to breathe anymore   some how/somehow
it still feels like you are in this
vas space of consciousness
deep
s   vas space of consciousness

so alone so alone so alone

this room
that goes
so deep
down this
hallow pathway
feels like you
are floating in this
nnneeevvvveeerrrr ending
room

of darkness and numbness

i wish this room had a light
a dim light

something for me to hold, need

something to hold on to

*its just dark.

but it just doesnt*

Flip Page
Forending.

Written by

August 28, 2020

fuck littt i aint got nothing to say, imma get fucked up like its my last day
no time to play lets get litty today
im alive im vibing im high off the ground
smash shit to the floor lifes a whore
get whats coming to you
you no good
dream door.

come out evevry day to play
to celabrate our movements
       from day to day
   welcome to our comunity
         the comunity that lies deep away
       counting down the love we share day to day

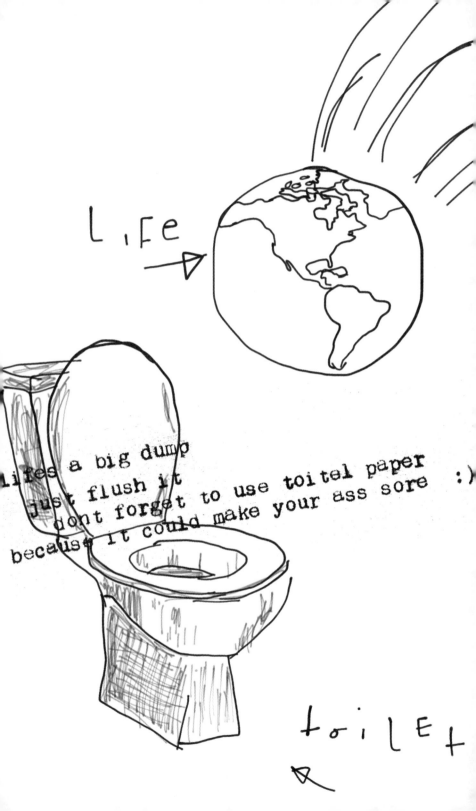

LiFe →

lifes a big dump
just flush it
dont forget to use toitel paper
because it could make your ass sore :)

toiLEt

daddy

whhhhhhh

Why did you leave? when will you be back? why wont you be at my wedding?

or my funeral ? they say a parent should h== never have to burry their child

~~his~~ but a child should never have 2 burry their dad either

even tho i didnt get to physically be there with you on the cold metal slab

i feel like i was. i saw the pictures. i was told how cold your skin felt

h described how you could feel the glass in your hair with the stitches from

your autopsy ... now i might not have been there at that moment in time

but theres quite a few moments. when i feel like im laying right next to you

on that cold metal brisk slab. right next to you

asking you questions , so many questions. questions that ill never have the answers 2

why is the question i keep asking over and over like this typewriter stuck on repeat

but i guess the better question is why..not?

why not me ? why would this pain be better for anyone else better for anyone else out

me ME ME ME

what a selfish thing 2 say and wish. i just wish it wasnt me

everything happens for a reason right? well i might be stuck searching for that

reason every single day for the rest of my life, so maybe its better to stop now

stop asking questions that i know ill never have the answers to

and if i had the answers would that help me? would that make me cry a little less?

probably not. i would prob-bly be sitting on this plane thinking, and crying, and

wondering. so is it better to just let go? let go completely, let you go,

release that ballon we do every yearin honnor of you or is it better to forget

forget thatballon forget about everything and just live god i need to live so fucking

so fucking bad.

i know you have to hurt and feel, feel the feelings you aren====
meant to feel. but what if..... what if those deep darkned feelings
what if those feelings are to hard to live in. to deep you know youll get
swallowed whole. like a catfish does to its prey or even
a snake.

maybe just forgetting and letting time take its nasty beautiful course
letting the whole thing go, maybe that,s the only thing that will help me
me move on, feeling the a pain, for a minute and then just pushing it out
letting it live alone in the dark where i never go .

in time daddy. in time.

death is lke this heavy rock
laying on you and theres this really
slow crain lifting this rock off you,
this crain is taking its sweet   time.
time is the crain

time = crain

RED MADNESS

Everything ridden with madness never has an
end. The spiral of madness twirls both ways.
The madness that seeks me, takes everything
good away. The madness creeps over me at
night holds me tight like sleep paralysis,
madness is that monster woman. She tears u a
part and keeps only the best parts for her-
self. Madness is unattainable if you have
boundaries. Unattainable madness does not
lie in those in restricted areas. Madness
can not live only in the dark but also the
light.

Madness needs balance like ice and fire Mad-
ness makes everything red.

Red madness red madness red madness RED MAD-
NESS RED MADNESS RED MADNESS RED MADNESS

Madness is a beautifully despicable place to
be,

where you will meet THE 3.

Madness of 3 the only place to be.

The 3 seek me, I can feel them coming for me

Red madness red madness

RIDDEN WITH RED MADNESS

there.   im standing right

where you left me

and now im stuck here. i dont know
where i am anymore.
theres a turn here and a corner there

up where that oil slick is,

are your thoughts left there??

WORTHY

somethings thats really tickling

me up my sweater sleeves.

is how women are being taught to veiw themself

today in our society. as you know it were being

taught to veiw ~~themself~~ our selves based on looks

body and hair and nails..worst part is its not even

based on our own opinion but the opinions of others.

letting these opinions of others deteriam who we should grow up and be

or how worthy we are. worthy of what? is my question what are we not

worthy of? is it the big house , is it the boy who sits next to

you in class? or is it the mean girls who constaly gabber

crude, crull coments to you when you walk past.

which you are not worthy of? what are we trying to be worthy for?

not ready to show compassion for ourthers and especially not

to to ~~our sleves~~

ourselves. so lets start small really small..dont make me

do all the work. think, really ponder to yourself, how can

you show a bit more compassion to others? also, more importantly

showing yourself, how to look in the mirror and love YOU.

fight for beauty against chaos
_ i heard that somewhere.

                    i believe every
        no te~~_desevers~~--
              deserves to play
        wi th eacho ther
                6   --
                    mod sun

Pride

Pride
I wish I wasn t in a box
I wish they would
Let me fly
I wish they could see how beautiful all the colors
are up here in the sky.
The big and shiny and bright ones, their all the
things I love.
I wish they could feel the radiance that exudes
thru me from being my most self.
I guess I didn t think this thru
Why they wouldn t love me.. or you?
I wish they could understand why me and not she or
he or them. That this is my desison of who I am.
I wish they could see me
With a lidless box. I wish they could see me.
Maybe not today or tomorrow
Maybe when they do time will stop
And then I ll be free of this disgusting box.

HATE

over   im not crying anymore

over you . i just wanna
curl up in a ball sometimes and cry
just cry it all out but theres just too
much it just keeps spiolling out of me
                                    and
me. my tear ducts are sore.   and my

mind is onstantly racing w thoughts of you

but ill teach myself to stop, thats what i
i have to do. they say the only way to hate is
through loving first. well i guess i must love you
so much because i hate you so much. you never
cared , you were always a peice of shit. and you
still are. and i hope you never change so i
can never love you again. not only did you try

and hurt me , it was that reaction that you
needed. those heavy fucking tears spilling out
my eyes, thats what you needed. when i was

down you kicked harder, when i was up you
pulled the curtians down. down further, and further
to the core of the earth. even after i put myself
down for you over and over , so you could shine
brighter, you never returned the favor.
you fucking dick. almost like making me feel

terrible   just made you feel stronger . bigger
once a hourse horse now a stallion.
btw all your friends felt bad for me because

they kne   t
          w you so damn well.

because they new you so d[

damn well. through the ringer   once   again

your eyes making me wanna get you theraphy,
your jaw line makes me ~~nautious~~ nauseous
your
      nose ~~youused~~ to remind me of all the good
   parts of my father and now it just reminds me
all the cheating scum stories i have heard

about him... you promised to never hurt me
and i begged you not to make a promise you
cant keep. even then when i was inlove with u
   i knew what you were going todo to me, yet
{ stupid little girls stay.} you used to tell
    me you didnt relize all the shit you said
was so hurtful, but i know ~~know~~ now, that
     was your faveorite part. blood sucking
    prick. so im done.

          im done looking at your tagged photo
   on insta & im done talking about our cute
moments & im sure the fuck done crying over
your entitled ass. none of the pain i went
through!/ g oing   through is worth you
          you arent worthy of my pain
          you sick fuck.

Love

im so so sorry.

im not sure what to say besides i fucked up.
bad.
ill never for give myself. this day will
always taunt me. i have this mistake close to
my heart and ill never live it down.
my childish ways worked against me.

i believe you when you say you love me. i do

i promise i do. its just hard for me to let
go of the past. all those dark memories stored
way back there. everytime in the past when
someone has spoken those same exact words
that you just did. they lied to me, they broke
me , they fucked me. they fucked me into this
oblivion of doubt. so yeah i have my own
trust issues to move past. i should have

never put that on you baby. i can carry my
own baggadee- baggage. its heavy but thats
why i have ~~tu~~ hands. as to speak for my
se~~n~~ seativity. sensitivity. you know
where all that comes from.
i was never enough for her. i have
been so beaten down by her i dont know how

to stand straight. but none of that has any
thing to do with you.

i know we are both fucked up and somehow
we crave the pain. you are helping me
some of my issues. i couldnt be happier
have you here. here with me.

i admire you in so many
ways baby. and i wouldnt even be singing
if you didnt tell me my voice sounded beatuiful
in the car singing to that the used track
we love. the ground you ~ walk on is shaky
so lets go steady. my heart my soul, my music

all this ~ shit you g o through where you
hate yourself i get it. trust me i do.

this self doubt is exhuasting so let me
take that for you. im strong enough for two.

i could hate you and yet i would still love
you. you are never alone. i know you feel
that urge to runaway from anything good becau
thats how we were taught to love

stick around for the bad stuff we desevei
it, runaway from the good stuff ,
its too good to be true.

cause thats what love is right?
well not ours.

the demons are amoung us
say call your mom
your
sorry

even
if you arent
say your sorry

/\

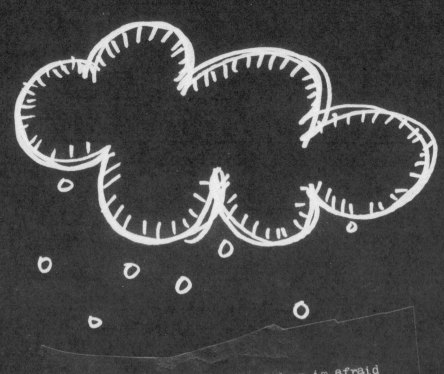

i feel so numb and deep im afraid
my heart might freeze..

your words are nothing
but ice cream cones
on the chopping block
waiting to be

devoured.

A love note to my mother

I love you mother.
I love some things about us.
Hmmmmmm.....
I'm not sure what to say
Usually my words
They come out w meaning
I used to be so lost in our relationship I never understood
it.
I don't
think I ever will
But what I do understand is everything u have left me with.
Which is so much, but almost nothing of myself
All the things I wish didn't happen are stupid Because they
made me who I am.
But then again who am I?
Who did you make mother?
Do you even know her ? Or understand the countless pain that
she still suffers with.
Do u know how angry I am
How angry I was.
I'm not angry anymore or at least I try not to be I try to
forgive and forget But then all the memories
come back with even
more questions then before.
I wish u saw me.
Saw us. Dani remy kaili
I wish u saw all we ever
really needed was you..
Now I'll never know what a mother is suppose to be or act or
how they are suppose to show love. I just
want you to know to know these
things.
I hope you know we never learned how to love Or at least I
never did. I learned love from you and daddy
but since he was gone mostly from you.
And I want you to know it's very hard for me to love properly
, to love someone good to me I want you

to know it's hard to make eye contact when someone
compliments me I want you to know When I make
love visions haunt me.

I want you to know
I'll always feel stupid even if I'm smart I want you to know I
want you to know I'll never look in the
mirror
and like what you have given me.
I want you to know
I'll never know if I'm a good mother
I want you to KNOW
I'll spend my whole life re learning
Re teaching myself
Undoing everything you have taught me.

when wrong is right
where do you turn
to catch the light.

black and blue.
    black is true
its the only color i feel
    when im with you

you beautiful peice of work

i dont want to be with

somebody   who wants constant change of me.

for Me to breathe in, and exhale unfamiliar teretor-ey.

i dont ask for this kind of atteion.

i cant live with a person who brings in so much

negativty   under a household roof.
so i still think i shoulant move in and i shoula
get my own living quarters. i have to try and find this happiness
on my own,..
you making your own self miserable worrying about so
much of my shit we arent spending so much, for the time

thats lost. im ok with that. but the constant

day dreaming of this life you think suits you.....
it doesnt suit me. im not the blonde with the clean

sheets and the oven on preheat. my life i never imagined

it to be tame or picture pictur perfct worthy.
as for that older figure i crave, it would be wrong of me
to put that weight on you , when youv cracked.
this burden and heavy responseabilty

its too big and so deep.
im sorry you felt obligated
you said that last night even after everything you still wanted
to make us work. gotta love a fighter, but now today you have
changed
yours opinion once again talk about stable endings.
i really under estimated this who juls hole.
i didnt think it was going to be this dep- deep.
i never wanted to hurt you like that. i just was angry.

i know how you feel about it, and again im sorry.
knew its all so damaqged but sometimes damage is good or

----perph perp -perao peraphs damge is needed. all ends
all ends content in time.

Ever wondered why money smells like old people Dead
presidents

I love vintage

Wearing someone else's

Memories and their own fiction

happiness i swear it will be mine
it might not be dripped in gold
but its a rare dime. happiness
would wash judgement away. so
that i could truly live in
this moment right away.

i worry my treasure is wrapped
in snakes and hidden far away

or that its right in front of
me and im too human to see it

so i ask you,

have

my   you   seen
   tr
      ea
      sure?

ha
 e
hsave you seen my happiness?
        oh is it right there?

    under your shoe?

        you cunt rag.

i dont work with

the odds
i work against them.

my special friend kyra

K: kick ass
Y: YOUphoric
R: relentless
A: addictive

at the center of the flash
is a black hole

sunshine

its obvious the sun is this outsourcing light

of energy.. and i mean energy in every sense
and yet, i kind of feel bad for that star..
   it had its own life, its own feelings,

   fuck it probably had its own grocery shoppin

list, and now we have stolen it away all for

   ourselves. keeping it so it could keep
   shining on us for all eternity..

now the sun is stuck with us, worrying
   if it goes aaway so might we?
   thats a lot of pressure for a poor little
star, out its so beautiful i need it

   all to myself, i cant stop wishing it
to never go away aand stay with us forever

so we might not a dark day. the sun
   it also feels as its obsorbing me.
            in.com pletely.

its keeping me alive, its fueling me with

   light, and radiance, its keeping me breathin

   and keeping my spirts high, high above the
ground, not to sink 6 feet below like how i

feel when the sun goes away.

or if its stormy at night, thats when

all my inner creatures come out to bite

they live inside me scratching

to get out...

but the sun keeps the light

inside me bright

and hides them far away

way, way out.

thats ↑
A SUN

Drag me up for air

You are so mean. I never thought we would
get to this ever and I m not sure how we
did. Break up over text after two years.
While I m dealing w the sacriest moments, u
steal my own words and tell them to my moth-
er in the worst ways and lie about what I
say after u know I needed to talk to her so
I could move past some of these awful ex-
periences in my life. And u take that RIGHT
FROM ME. You take my own words and spill
them terribly ridden with more darkness. I
can t even talk to her about it because of
u now. Just like u took CH from me, when it
was suppose to be about my father and YOU
made it about money and why aren t u be-
ing paid when I wasn t even being paid. If u
ever were a good boyfriend u would know u do
this shit on the ANNIVERSARY OF MY FATHERS
DEATH. but u don t realize that do u because
u are so self absorbed. I have been throw-
ing up every other hour crying at any point
on the day THIS IS WHEN I NEEDED U. This is
when 2 years is worth it because when the
waters are rough ur partner is suppose to
paddle with you. But u don t paddle w me. U
would rather watch me sink into the ocean
and drown just MOMENTs before u drag me up
for air. So U can save me. Instead of never
letting me sink in the first place.

Drag me up for air

debating is the best form of

a conversation

Greatful

I'm greatful for life

I'm greatful for the Lemonds still growing on the trees even after all we have put nature through.

I'm greatful that I'm writing this book and I even have a chance for someone to read this book other than myself One thing I know I'll never be greatful enough For is my sister.

I'm sorry if you're reading this and you don't have a sister or you aren't close w yours.

Everything I have I simply want to give it to her Because nothing will ever be compare to the emotional stability she has given me.

I know I could be anywhere.

I could be so fucked up.

Well I am fucked up.

But I could be throwing my life away is what I mean I could always let my past haunt me Let my past make my next desison But I don't.

Because my sister is standing right there Waiting on the other side of that rainbow.

Ushering me over

Showing me all the beautiful colors in life That are there... we just have to open our eyes and see them.

I don't really understand how she became so Smart and mature.

I'm pretty sure I'll always wonder.

But what I do know is how lost I would be without her hands prying my eyes open to see what's right in front of me.

I think life would almost be meaningless without finding your other half.

And finding that so early in life

Knowing that other half was in your life this whole time...

That is something I will always be greatful for.

the person who loves you most will always

take your best photograph

i heard that somewhere.......

                regrets are   the smartest most

        needed things, can live with them

        but cant live without em.

            i wanna say we should live regret free..

        all these regrets they hold us back

            they keep us trapped in the past, like

                    photographs. like polarizeds

                on a clipboard,

            so quickly to be forgotten about but

                when remereder ,

                    so harshly vivid ,
                        it stills you.
            that we should move from the past to

        the present. but how can we really ape
        apreciate the prsent , with out the
            fualities of the past....

                            all these

        vairiables seem so needed . almost like

        a left shoe, with out a right one.

            i feel so lost with out my regrets no idea

            how to feel about my future events..
        if you take a goldfish out of water,

            watch it slowly suffocate to death,
            and knowing you have all the power to
                save that sweet little goldfish.. ━

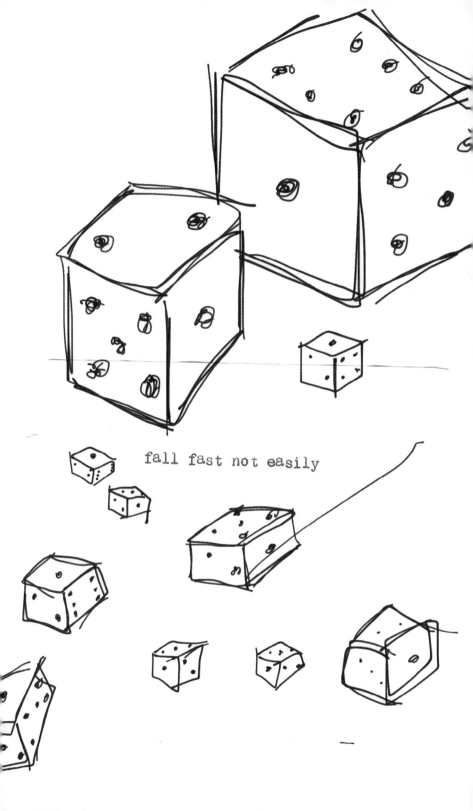

fall fast not easily

br   brooooooooooo the 20s were so

            ill , i miss those days....

once a snitch forever
        lies in a ditch

i screamed so hard today

i thought my throat would collasp

i felt my whole body come to this head.

this point that every cell in my body
was telling my brian to crack,

or maybe freeze,

or have a mofuncution

my whole body everything inside me

just stopped. and let go.

letting go into these retchet
screams. these blood cruddling
screams. i cracked, i broke
in every sense of the words,

i lost my shit.

so now i have to go pick my shit up
off the walls,

excuse me,

TRUE LOVE?

Little Bell

maybe one day, I'll give her a ring

alexa
B +

you bright and shiny girl
  you have dedicated your life to being
filled with darkness on most days
       i   appreciate you
    all you have done for the world,
            for the little girls and boys
                today
how you refuse to let that darkness
                dim thier days.

  you are so strong
       so brave
    im so proud of you
                have a good day:)

coincidences are for losers
dont be a pussy
     look
its right in front of u

whats better than angry and british
hahaha

self deprecation

is lost within me

i use it, to make others laugh about me

but dont worry i laugh on the inside

while i await my next move

self deprecation

is my mood, i use it to hide my true

intenions, so youll never see coming

my next moves.

self deprecating peice of shit.

regrets part 2

so back to ~~t~~ what i~~f~~ was saying about

regrets.

so after you suffocate that sweet innocent

little gold fish...

you what? / you FEEL BAD. / you,

regret it, you see.   you

you regret every dession that brought ~~me~~

to the death of a sweet goldfish

now if you hadnt made this, you might call

this, it a mistake,

this mistake . maybe you wouldnt have

learned the meaning of empathy.

now maybe this sudden empathy fuels you,

teachs you. never leaves your side,

forever huanting your thoughts,

and constantly reminding you of this

person tha t lies within you,

that you need to change.

regerts . these ficikle funny

little things...

regrets they hold you back,

or they push you forward.

pushing you to strive, to never

be again, what you once were.
let your regets push you foward

feel them when they are needed

to be felt.
dont push them down or hide them away

let them pick you up and remind
you to make (a) different desicon today

-me

do me a favor,

ask your friends,
        or your parents,
                or your   co people,
    what do they regret?

then maybe once knowing someones
    darker places we can appreciate,

            thier light ones.

2/2

FUCKING SHAKESPEARE HE REALLY

COCKED ME OUTTA LOVE!!!!!!!!!
!!
!!
!!!!!!!!!!!!!!!!!!!!!!!!!!!!!!!!!!
!!!!!!!!!!!!!!!!!!!!!

!!!!!!!!!!   !!!!!!!!!!!!!!!!!!!!!!!
!!!!!!!!!!!!!!!!!!!!!!!

believe in your highness
and concour your ~~shiness~~
shi_ ness

— mod sun

runaway daddy..

verse;
junked up with nothing to say
fuckup, its time ~~tp~~ to pay
worked up its your last day
  now pay with ur life because its
      time to stay

    chorus;
daddy daddy,
 i wish you would come find me
     daddy daddy
it doesnt hurt when itsyou and me
     daddy daddy
when you walked out the door, i didnt know
   i was petrified, but i woulant let you
       see me cry
lived your life in the fast lane
    too bad its caused us all this pain.
from streets to fame with nothing to gain
  you left me outside, wondering in the rair
      daddy daddy
please dont make me cry
     daddy daddy
       lets just ride

1/2

verse 2;

wondering how you got this way

bleeding out with no one around

bleeding out, peep dont make a sound

lets try this again but the right way

maybe this time youll stay??

bridge:

daddy daddy

now your in a hole

daddy daddy

lying ~~there~~ Lying there oh so cold

daddy daddy

bugs surrounding your heart

daddy daddy lying in the dark

daddy daddy stand up

daddy daddy man up

dont get me wrong my dad was a good man

sometimes life doesnt work out as planned

daddy daddy lying ~~t~~ in the dark

daddy da day peace around your heart.

never one foot in

all four limbs

all limbs at all times

its g GO time.

green light

this life is unreal

sometimes i cant deal

cant deal
i wish that i could unfeel
unfeel

the scale isnt your answer

your incredulous self doubt

is your anwser.

dear, fellow person wi th ~~body dysmorph~~

body— dysmorphia.

all   all these sad girl written pages,

yeah im sick of it to,

but i try to look at the beautiful things

in life, you may interpet them AS dark

or lost,

things.

but i think they are darkley beautiful

things.

like when your driving for awhile for and

your really getting sick of this constant

never ending road, and you start to get

anxious,.

i stare at the red lights on the backs of

cars. i love red

i love the color red

i like red things

even this book is red.

and i like whit— the white lights on the

opposite side of the freeway too.

i dont love em. im not obbsessed with em

, the color white i mean, but ill take em.

whites kinda pretty

i like white roses, theyer ok.

red and

red and white thats what the cars

in traffic look like

red and white lights

just like
christmas lights
i love christmas

i love the whole idea behind christmas.

the family love

the family loyalty

even through harsh times, still

finding thier way back to eachother,

the hot choclate,

the relishing in old story telling.
christmas is full of joy these days, but

i still feel sad

cant help it.
but the essence of christmas i love.

so the ugly things in life dont always

have to be so ugly. if you search far enough

down that dark lonely room.

im sure youll find

rde red and white christmas lights.

faveoriute songs to this day
so far..

people are strange - the doors

crimson and clovers - joan jett
white wedding-billy ~~savere~~ idol

tainted love - the cure
whats real - WATERS

HIGH WAY TO HELL= ACDC
gonorrhea - lil wayne

all that iv got- the used

welcome to the-~~gun~~-- jungle- guns n roses

the beautiful people - marylin manson
clint eastwood - gorillaz

$6 foot 7 foot - lil wayne
riptide - vance joy
paridice citty - guns n roses

closer-nine inch nails
get your freak on -- missy elliottt

tnt - ACDC
hea-   crazy on you - heart
nu... ...inkin park
...ly squier

My neocortex holds my
Everything
Everything about me that makes me ok
It's all this one tiny little thing
So, what if we Shut that tiny little
thing off
Completely.
Eject
Terminate
Dewire
Unplug
Detach.
Delete
  good bye
What would become of us then?
Would we be savages ?
Relying on completely
Instinct fear and aggression
Would that be what we really are down to
our core
Without our control center
Just our core.
Just animals,
Or more importantly
savages.

yup ,

hes a murder,

it smells like bodies down

here

fairygodmother;

ever lasting innocents

   lies within us,

time is of no relevance here,

     my dear,
because ever lasting

       innocents

          lies within
        us

     my beautiful queer.

some of the best

things are done rushed.

you know when andy says to ~~red~~ red,

" its funny. on the outside,

i was an honest man.
straight as an arrow.

i had to come to

prison to ~~be~~ be a

a crook."

something about those words
rang 2 deep
go back up, read it again.

now really think about it...

— the shawshank redemption

Daniella Morgan thorne

No words could do justice for the
love I have invested in you.

I simply love everything you do

my loops are long andtendinouis
they are long like vines , they are slighty
~~b- ripped-~~ rippled like that sea of
drowning memories washing over your good nights
sleep. these long ropes you might describe

as my ~~libe-~~ limbs . i would describe   ,

what a tentacle is to an octopus,
or a branch to a tree.

my glass mask is bubbled in ro und ways
you cant imagine, very much marbled like
those shiny floors. seek me for pleasure,
i have many different outputs for your liking
try my different holes, they fit many tubes.
if half ed of me is with out a tube,
how will I breathe and work for me but mostly
for you?

1/2

you can suck me dry,of all my juice

and exhale my inner workings, careful
that cough might bruise.

   troubled moments await my future.

     those crude beings might shatter me
           with out a flinch.
good thing you mostly keep me hidden
in that dark lonely closet,so your
rentswont steal   a glance

i have traveled a very long time through
   time, just to end up at a shop near you.

     the best part is
  youll still use me even when im
    tattered and no longer new.

See next
page,4
answer 2/2

what am i ???

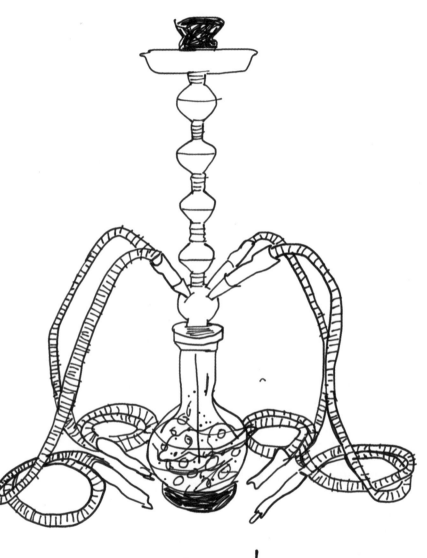

I'M A HOOKAH

If you don't know it learn it
Learn it
Love it
Strive with it
Forget it
Learn it again
And again
until u know it
And the moment u know it
Stop

because you'll never know it fully
Once you think you have learned everything u have
started back at square one And now you have learned
nothing.
There is no roof
There is not celling
The box doesn't have a top
The box is lid less
Now learn it again.

the chills dont ~~y~~

have a fucking genre.

Dear Mother,

I'm sorry for the words
I have said.
I needed to get them
out, from lingering
underneath my skin...
I know your life hasn't
Been perfect and
I know thats why mine
hasnt either.
everythin in life is a mystery
But what isnt is this infinite
undying love I have 4 you.
our relationship is fucked up but I'm glad
you are here. I'm greatful we have time to men
I love you mommy.

"You'll always be the Cece to my Rocky."

—Zendaya

"Yo, sitting here smokin', checking out this book of poems from my homegirl Bella. Damn girl, you dope as a mothafucka. I didn't know you had rhymes and rhythms and such words of magnitude and gratitude with just a little bit of attitude. Yes, make sure you go get that book from my homegirl Bella. Book of rhymes certified so says Snoop Dogg. Oh yeah, she's a poet and she know it and she ain't afraid to show it. And if you happy and you know it, BLOW it. This for you, Bella, do ya shit girl!!"

—Snoop Dogg

"Bella Thorne is raw in every sense of the word: tender, juicy, bloody, revealed. Nobody does what she does, which is tell us how the fuck she feels and that it's okay to fucking feel it. I honor her."

—Lena Dunham

Definition of quote in English (*Oxford English Dictionary*):
QUOTE

VERB

[WITH OBJECT]

1 Repeat or copy out (words from a text or speech written or spoken by another person)
'I realized she was quoting passages from Shakespeare'
[no object] 'he quoted from the scriptures'
1.1 Repeat a statement by (someone)
'a military spokesman was quoted as saying that the border was now quiet'
1.2 Mention or refer to (someone or something) to provide evidence
or authority for a statement or opinion.
'the examples quoted above could be multiplied from case studies
from all over England'
1.3 (**quote someone/something as**)
Put forward or describe someone or something as being.
'heavy teaching loads are often quoted as a bad influence on research'

2 Give someone (the estimated price of a job or service)
[with two objects] 'a garage quoted him £30'
2.1 (**quote someone/something at/as**) Name at (specified odds)
'he is quoted as 9–2 favourite to score the first goal of the match'

3 *Stock Market*
Give (a company) a quotation or listing on a stock exchange.
'a British conglomerate quoted on the London Stock Exchange'

NOUN

1. A quotation from a text or speech.
'a quote from Wordsworth'

2. A quotation giving the estimated cost for a particular job or service.
'quotes from different insurance companies'

2.1 *Stock Market* A price offered by a market-maker for the sale
or purchase of a stock or other security.
'*quotes for North Sea Brent were rising*'

3 *Stock Market*
A quotation or listing of a company on a stock exchange.

4 (**quotes**) Quotation marks.
'*use double quotes around precise phrases you wish to search for*'

PHRASES

quote—unquote (also quote, unquote)
informal Used parenthetically when speaking to indicate the beginning
and end of a statement or passage that one is repeating.
'*the second sentence says, quote, There has never been a better time
to invest in the commodities market, unquote*'
'*the brochure describes the view as, quote, unquote, unforgettably breathtaking*'

ORIGIN

Late Middle English: from medieval Latin quotare, from quot 'how many', or
from medieval Latin quota (see quota). The original sense was 'mark a book
with numbers, or with marginal references', later 'give a reference by page or
chapter', hence 'cite a text or person' (late 16th century).

"This is a quote for a book of poems by Bella Thorne."

—Jared Leto

"Hey, I didn't read this book. Bella gave it to me and I left it on an airplane."

—Diplo

"Bella is one of those rare artists who is utterly fearless. Her courage to show you who she truly is—including hopes, fears, and vulnerabilities—is what makes her a relevant and meaningful voice for this generation."

—Scott Spear

"Bella Thorne writes poetry as a kidnapper might leave a ransom note. It's a threat. And I don't think she's fucking around."

—Jason Reitman

"Bella…is like an opened Pandora's box! Endlessly overflowing with golden delight and darkest seriousness. Your life could be altered if she catches your eye."

—Melissa Leo

"I haven't read Bella's book, but if it's anything like her then you're in for a treat. She's honest like so few are these days. She's a rule breaker. Doesn't stay in her lane. Pushes herself beyond what you'd expect. She misbehaves. Doesn't follow the rules. I love her for all of that. All women could benefit from behaving a little less. It's an exciting prospect right?"

—Jessica Chastain